nature's
baby animals

BABY ANIMALS
OF THE WETLANDS

Carmen Bredeson

Dennis L. Claussen, PhD, *Series Science Consultant* Professor of Zoology, Miami University, Oxford, Ohio

Allan A. De Fina, PhD, *Series Literacy Consultant* Dean, College of Education/Department of Literacy Education, New Jersey City University, Jersey City, New Jersey; Past President of the NJ Reading Association

CONTENTS

WORDS TO KNOW

hatchling (HATCH ling)—A baby born from an egg.

marsh (marsh)—Land that is covered with water most of the time. It has plants like tall grasses.

swamp (swahmp)—Land that is covered with water most of the time. It has plants like shrubs and trees.

webbed (webd)—Joined by a piece of skin (such as fingers or toes).

3

WETLANDS

A wetland is land that has a lot of water.

A **swamp** is a wetland.

A **marsh** is a wetland.

Some wetlands have fresh water.

Others have salt water.

Baby animals have special ways to stay

safe and live in a wetland.

BABY WOOD DUCK

Wood ducks are born in a nest high in a tree. When the ducks are one day old, they jump out of the nest. DOWN, DOWN they fall. *Splash!* Their mother is waiting in the water for her babies.

A baby wood duck jumps to the water.

Baby alligators hatch from eggs.
Their mother carries them to water in her
MOUTH! The little alligators crawl onto
their mother's head. She keeps them safe
from hungry fish, snakes, and raccoons.

**BABY
ALLIGATOR**

BABY SANDHILL CRANE

This chick is one day old.

Baby sandhill cranes are called colts.

They can walk right after they are born.

The babies follow their parents onto the marsh.

The parents feed the colts bugs and plants.

Soon the colts will find food on their own.

Nutria [NOO tree uh] spend a lot of time in the water. Nutria babies ride on their parents' backs while they swim.

Soon the babies learn to swim on their own. Their **webbed** back toes help them move through the water.

BABY **NUTRIA**

BABY EGRET

Egret [EE gret] chicks are very hungry!
Both parents bring food to the chicks.
Egrets stand very still on long legs.
They stab fish and frogs with their
sharp bills.

Turtle **hatchlings** break out of their eggs. They go to the marsh grass to find food. The little turtles eat insects, worms, and plants. When danger is near, they jump into the water and hide in the mud.

BABY TURTLE

These are spotted turtles.

BABY PANTHER

Florida panther kittens are born in a warm den near the swamp. The kittens grow hair that has dark spots on it. Their fur helps them hide in the grass and plants. The kittens can stay safe from enemies.

old shell

A dragonfly hatches from an egg in the water. It breathes through gills like a fish. One day it walks onto land. It crawls out of its old skin. Now it can spread its wings and fly.

This dragonfly just crawled out of its shell.

BABY DRAGONFLY

Learn More

Books

Aloian, Molly, and Bobbie Kalman. *A Wetland Habitat*. New York: Crabtree Publishing Co., 2006.

Arnosky, Jim. *All About Turtles*. New York: Scholastic, Inc., 2008.

Caper, William. *Florida Panthers: Struggle for Survival*. New York: Bearport Publishing, 2008.

Lion, David C. *A Home in the Swamp*. New York: Children's Press, 2006.

Twine, Alice. *Alligators*. New York: PowerKids Press, 2008.

Enchanted Learning
<http://www.enchantedlearning.com/biomes/swamp/
swamp.shtml>

*Learn about swamp animals with games
and activities.*

National Geographic
<http://kids.nationalgeographic.com/Animals/
CreatureFeature/American-alligator>

*Watch a video of alligators
and hear what sound they make.*

INDEX

~For Kate and Caroline, our beautiful granddaughters~

Enslow Elementary, an imprint of Enslow Publihshers, Inc.
Enslow Elementary® is a registered trademark of Enslow Publishers, Inc.

Library of Congress Cataloging-in-Publication Data

Bredeson, Carmen.
  Baby animals of the wetlands / Carmen Bredeson.
    p. cm. — (Nature's baby animals)
  Includes bibliographical references and index.
  Summary: "Up-close photos and information about baby animals of the wetlands"—
Provided by publisher.
  Library Ed. ISBN 978-0-7660-3564-5
  Paperback ISBN 978-1-59845-227-3
  1. Wetland animals—Infancy—Juvenile literature. I. Title.
  QL113.8.B74 2011
  591.768—dc22

                                    2009037900

Printed in the United States of America
102010 Lake Book Manufacturing, Inc., Melrose Park, IL

10 9 8 7 6 5 4 3 2 1

To Our Readers: We have done our best to make sure all Internet Addresses in this book were active and appropriate when we went to press. However, the author and the publisher have no control over and assume no liability for the material available on those Internet sites or on other Web sites they may link to. Any comments or suggestions can be sent by e-mail to comments@enslow.com or to the address on the back cover.

Enslow Publishers, Inc., is committed to printing our books on recycled paper. The paper in every book contains 10% to 30% post-consumer waste (PCW). The cover board on the outside of each book contains 100% PCW. Our goal is to do our part to help young people and the environment too!

Every effort has been made to locate all copyright holders of material used in this book. If any errors or omissions have occurred, corrections will be made in future editions of this book.

Photo Credits: © Dale Jackson/Visuals Unlimited, p. 3 (hatchling); © Duncan Usher/ Minden Pictures, p. 20; © James Carmichael Jr./NHPA, pp. 1, 9; © James Urbach/ photolibrary.com, p. 10; © Jeff Cashdollar/iStockphoto.com, pp. 2 (left), 14; © Jim Merli/ Visuals Unlimited, Inc., pp. 16, 23; © John Cancalosi/Alamy, p. 15; © Karen Massier/ iStockphoto.com, p. 5; © Kennan Ward 2010, p. 19; © Leszczynski, Zigmund/Animals Animals, p. 17; © Lockwood, C.C./Animals Animals, p. 8; © McDonald Wildlife Photog/ Animals Animals, p. 7; © National Geographic/Getty Images, p. 11; © Ralph Arwood/DRK Photo, p. 18; © Rene Krekels/Foto Natura/Minden Pictures, p. 21; © Roberto Cerruti/ iStockphoto.com, p. 12; Shutterstock, p. 3 (marsh, swamp, webbed); © T Kitchin & V Hurst/ NHPA, p. 6; © Wildlife/Peter Arnold Inc., pp. 2 (right), 13.

Cover Photo: © James Carmichael Jr./NHPA

Note to Parents and Teachers: The *Nature's Baby Animals* series supports the National Science Education Standards for K–4 science. The Words to Know section introduces subject-specific vocabulary words, including pronunciation and definitions. Early readers may need help with these new words.

Enslow Elementary
an imprint of
Enslow Publishers, Inc.
40 Industrial Road
Box 398
Berkeley Heights, NJ 07922
USA
http://www.enslow.com